I0019747

Understanding Human Ingenuity and Machine Prowess: The Age of Artificial Intelligence: A roadmap through the circuits and algorithms that propel us into an uncharted future.

By

Daveson Wright

Disclaimer:

The material presented in "Understanding Human Ingenuity and Machine Prowess: The Age of Artificial Intelligence: A roadmap through the circuits and algorithms that propel us into an uncharted future." is meant for general guidance and instructional purposes only. It should not be considered a substitute for professional guidance or instruction from a trained expert. The author and publisher disclaim any duty for any damages or injuries resulting from the application or misapplication of the material included in this book. Always contact a professional when dealing with specific technical difficulties or project concerns.

Table of Contents

INTRODUCTION

In the span of a few decades, humanity has witnessed an unprecedented transformation—a revolution not in the physical realm, but in the boundless landscape of intelligence. We stand on the precipice of an era defined by the synthesis of human ingenuity and machine prowess—the Age of Artificial Intelligence.

As we navigate this landscape, the contours of our world are being reshaped, redefined, and, at times, refracted through the lens of algorithms and neural networks. The Age of AI is not merely a technological epoch; it is a paradigm shift that touches the very essence of what it means to be human.

It extends beyond the confines of computer labs and research institutions, weaving its threads through the fabric of our societies, economies, and daily lives. This book endeavors to be both a guide and a contemplation—a roadmap through the circuits and algorithms that propel us into an uncharted future, and a reflective pause to ponder the implications of our journey.

As we embark on this exploration, we will trace the historical footprints of artificial intelligence, from the conceptual musings of Alan Turing to the neural networks that now echo the intricacies of the human brain. Through the corridors of time, we will encounter the milestones that have shaped this evolution—expert systems, machine learning, and the profound emergence of deep learning architectures.

Yet, the narrative goes beyond the technological chronicle; it delves into the profound impact of AI on industries, from the renaissance in healthcare to the algorithmic symphonies of financial markets and the metamorphosis of manufacturing through automation.

But the Age of AI is not just about algorithms and data; it is about us—our values, ethics, and the societal tapestry that binds us together. Ethical considerations loom large as we grapple with questions of bias, privacy, and the complex interplay between man and machine. We explore the nexus of AI and employment, contemplating the waves of disruption and the shores of opportunity that reshape the workforce landscape.

As we navigate the landscape of this new era, we will uncover the potential of human-AI collaboration—where machines augment human capabilities and humans guide the evolution of artificial intelligence. The book paints a portrait of a future where responsible AI practices and international collaboration form the backbone of governance, and we speculate on the technological singularities that might lie on the horizon.

The Age of AI is a call to action and reflection. It invites us to not only witness the unfolding chapters of this narrative but to actively participate in shaping its trajectory.

This book is an invitation to the curious, the contemplative, and the visionary—to those who seek not only to understand the algorithms that define our future but to envision the broader canvas of our human journey as we step boldly into the embrace of artificial intelligence.

Definition and Evolution of AI

The Genesis of Artificial Intelligence

In the annals of human thought, the concept of machines endowed with intelligence has roots that extend far beyond the silicon age.

From the ancient myths of automatons to the philosophical inquiries of the Enlightenment, the idea of replicating cognitive functions in non-biological entities has tantalized the human imagination. The seeds of artificial intelligence were planted in the fertile soil of human curiosity and the pursuit of knowledge.

Defining Artificial Intelligence

As we embark on this exploration, a crucial question demands attention: What exactly is Artificial Intelligence? At its core, AI is the science and engineering of creating intelligent agents—systems that perceive their environment, reason about it, and take actions to achieve specific goals. This definition encompasses a spectrum of capabilities, from the rule-based logic of early AI systems to the neural networks driving the latest advancements in machine learning.

The Turing Test: A Milestone in Conceptualization

In 1950, Alan Turing, a pioneer in computing and cryptography, proposed a groundbreaking idea—an operational test for intelligence that would become a touchstone for AI.

The Turing Test, as it came to be known, posited that a machine could be considered intelligent if its responses were indistinguishable from those of a human during natural language interactions. This concept became a lodestar, guiding the trajectory of AI research for decades.

From Symbolic Logic to Expert Systems

The early years of AI were marked by the pursuit of symbolic reasoning, where researchers sought to encode human knowledge into systems using formal logic.

This era gave rise to expert systems—programs designed to mimic the decision-making abilities of a human expert in a specific domain. Despite notable successes, the limitations of symbolic AI soon became apparent, prompting a shift towards more data-driven approaches.

Machine Learning: A Quantum Leap

The evolution of AI took a quantum leap with the advent of machine learning. Rather than relying on explicit programming, machine learning algorithms enabled systems to learn from data and improve their performance over time.

From the foundational work of Arthur Samuel on gaming strategies to the development of decision trees and regression models, the landscape of AI was transformed, paving the way for more sophisticated learning architectures.

Neural Networks and the Resurgence of Deep Learning

In recent years, the resurgence of neural networks, inspired by the structure and function of the human brain, has propelled AI into new frontiers. Deep learning, a subfield of machine learning, involves neural networks with multiple layers (deep neural networks).

These architectures have demonstrated unparalleled success in tasks such as image recognition, natural language processing, and game playing, redefining the boundaries of what AI can achieve.

The Contemporary Landscape

Today, AI is an omnipresent force, permeating diverse facets of our lives. From voice-activated assistants to recommendation systems shaping our online experiences, the impact of AI is profound and multifaceted. The evolution of AI continues to unfold, fueled by advancements in hardware, algorithms, and the unprecedented availability of data.

Significance of the Age of AI

The Transformative Power

The Age of Artificial Intelligence heralds a transformative power that transcends the boundaries of technology. It is not merely a progression in algorithms or an evolution of hardware; it is a seismic shift that reverberates through the core of our societies, economies, and individual lives. Understanding the significance of this age requires a holistic examination of its impact on various dimensions of human existence.

Redefining Productivity and Efficiency

One of the paramount contributions of AI lies in its ability to redefine productivity and efficiency across industries. Automation, powered by intelligent algorithms and robotic systems, has streamlined processes, reduced errors, and optimized resource utilization. From manufacturing plants to service industries, the integration of AI has become synonymous with increased output and operational excellence.

Unleashing Creativity and Innovation

In the tapestry of human ingenuity, AI emerges as a catalytic thread, weaving through the fabric of creativity and innovation.

Machine learning algorithms, capable of identifying patterns and making predictions from vast datasets, serve as accelerators for scientific discovery, artistic expression, and the creation of novel solutions to complex problems. The collaborative dance between human intuition and machine intelligence opens new frontiers of possibility.

Revolutionizing Healthcare

The Age of AI holds particular significance in the realm of healthcare. From diagnostic tools that outperform human clinicians to personalized treatment plans tailored to individual genetic profiles, artificial intelligence is revolutionizing the way we understand and address medical challenges.

The marriage of data analytics, machine learning, and medical expertise promises a future where diseases are detected earlier, treatments are more precise, and healthcare delivery is optimized.

Redefining Human-Machine Interaction

As AI permeates our daily lives, the nature of human-machine interaction undergoes a profound redefinition. Voice-activated assistants, natural language processing, and gesture recognition systems are not just tools; they are companions and collaborators. The significance lies not only in the convenience they offer but in the evolving dynamics of how we communicate, work, and relate to the intelligent entities that share our spaces.

Economic Impacts and New Frontiers

The economic landscape is experiencing tectonic shifts as AI takes center stage. While concerns about job displacement persist, the Age of AI also unfolds new frontiers of economic opportunity.

Entrepreneurial ventures centered around AI applications, the rise of AI-driven industries, and the emergence of novel business models are reshaping the economic ecosystem. The significance of this era lies in the dynamic interplay between disruption and innovation.

Ethical Considerations and Societal Impact

Beyond the realms of productivity and economic shifts, the Age of AI raises profound ethical considerations. Bias in algorithms, concerns about privacy, and the potential for unintended consequences underscore the need for responsible AI development and deployment. The significance of this age is not solely in what AI enables but in how we navigate the ethical complexities to ensure that its benefits are justly distributed across diverse societies.

Purpose and Scope of the Book

Unveiling the Narrative Architecture

As we embark on this intellectual journey through the Age of AI, it is imperative to grasp the overarching purpose and scope that guide the narrative architecture of this book.

The purpose extends beyond mere elucidation; it is a quest to weave a tapestry that not only explains the intricacies of artificial intelligence but also prompts introspection and dialogue about its profound implications for our human future.

Enlightening the Inquisitive Mind

At its core, the purpose of this book is to enlighten the inquisitive mind. It seeks to cater to a diverse audience—ranging from technology enthusiasts and industry professionals to policymakers, ethicists, and the curious general reader.

The narrative is crafted with a dual mission: to provide a comprehensive understanding of AI's technological landscape and to stimulate contemplation on the broader ethical, societal, and existential dimensions it encompasses.

Navigating the Complex Terrain

The scope of the book extends far beyond a mere exploration of algorithms and neural networks. It encompasses the multidimensional facets of AI, from its historical roots to its contemporary applications and the speculative horizons of its future. The narrative threads weave through the corridors of technology, industry, ethics, and governance, providing a panoramic view of the landscape shaped by artificial intelligence.

Bridging the Gap between Expertise and Accessibility

In recognizing the diverse backgrounds and expertise of potential readers, the book aspires to bridge the gap between technical intricacies and accessibility. For those deeply entrenched in the world of AI, it offers nuanced insights and reflections that provoke thought. Simultaneously, for those less familiar with the technicalities, it provides lucid explanations and analogies, ensuring that the journey through the pages remains enriching and comprehensible.

Encouraging Informed Conversations

Beyond serving as a source of knowledge, the book is a catalyst for informed conversations. It aims to equip readers with the tools to engage in discussions about the societal, ethical, and policy dimensions of AI. By presenting a balanced exploration of the promises and perils of the Age of AI, the book encourages a nuanced discourse that transcends binary perspectives and embraces the complexity inherent in our relationship with artificial intelligence.

A Framework for Ethical Contemplation

Ethics is at the heart of the book's purpose. It seeks not only to highlight ethical considerations but also to provide a framework for ethical contemplation. As we navigate the uncharted territories of AI, the book encourages readers to reflect on the values that should guide the development and deployment of intelligent systems, ensuring that the benefits of AI are aligned with the principles of fairness, transparency, and accountability.

Empowering Decision-Makers

In an era where decisions about AI reverberate across boardrooms, legislative chambers, and research labs, the book serves as a resource for decision-makers. Whether shaping corporate strategies, formulating public policies, or contributing to the discourse surrounding responsible AI development, the insights contained within these pages aim to empower those with the agency to influence the trajectory of AI in our societies.

Historical Perspective

Early Developments in Artificial Intelligence

The journey into the historical roots of artificial intelligence takes us back to a time when the notion of machines emulating human intelligence was more fantasy than reality.

Turing's Contributions

At the forefront of early AI conceptualization stands the visionary figure of Alan Turing. Turing, a mathematician and logician, laid the cornerstone for the theoretical underpinnings of artificial intelligence. His seminal 1936 paper, "On Computable Numbers," introduced the concept of a theoretical computing machine—what we now know as the Turing machine. This conceptual framework not only became the theoretical foundation for modern computers but also served as a crucial precursor to the idea of artificial intelligence.

The Turing Test: A Pivotal Moment

Turing's influence on AI extends beyond theoretical constructs. In 1950, he proposed the Turing Test, a watershed moment in the history of artificial intelligence.

The test challenged the capacity of a machine to exhibit intelligent behavior indistinguishable from that of a human during natural language interactions. While the Turing Test remains a subject of philosophical debate, its introduction catalyzed discussions on the possibility of creating machines that could simulate human cognition.

Birth of Machine Learning

The quest to imbue machines with the ability to learn from data, a cornerstone of contemporary AI, finds its origins in the mid-20th century. In the 1940s and 1950s, the field of cybernetics, pioneered by Norbert

Wiener, explored the parallels between human and machine learning.

However, it was Arthur Samuel who brought machine learning into sharper focus. In 1959, he defined machine learning as a field of study that gives computers the ability to learn without being explicitly programmed. Samuel's work laid the groundwork for the development of algorithms capable of improving their performance through experience—a fundamental tenet of modern machine learning.

Early Machine Learning Algorithms

The birth of machine learning algorithms marked a paradigm shift in AI. One of the earliest practical applications emerged in the field of gaming, where Samuel's checkers-playing program demonstrated an ability to refine its strategy through repeated exposure to the game. This concept of learning through experience set the stage for the evolution of machine learning techniques, paving the way for more sophisticated algorithms in the decades to come.

The Dartmouth Conference: The Birth of AI as a Field

In the summer of 1956, a seminal event known as the Dartmouth Conference brought together pioneers such as John McCarthy, Marvin Minsky, and Claude Shannon, giving birth to AI as a distinct field of study.

The conference set the agenda for AI research, defining the goals and challenges that would shape the trajectory of the discipline. It marked the beginning of a concentrated effort to develop intelligent machines and laid the groundwork for subsequent decades of research and innovation.

Challenges and Ambitions

The early days of AI were characterized by ambitious aspirations and formidable challenges. The computational limitations of the time, coupled with nascent understanding of cognitive processes, posed significant obstacles.

Yet, the visionaries of this era laid the intellectual foundation for a discipline that would eventually transcend these challenges, shaping the landscape of artificial intelligence we navigate today.

Milestones in AI Evolution

As the tapestry of artificial intelligence continued to unfold, pivotal milestones emerged, marking significant advancements in the field. This chapter traces the trajectory of AI evolution through two key milestones: the development of expert systems and the resurgence of neural networks.

Expert Systems: The Knowledge-Based Approach

In the 1960s and 1970s, a paradigm shift occurred in AI research with the advent of expert systems. These systems aimed to capture and replicate the knowledge and reasoning abilities of human experts in specific domains.

The knowledge-based approach involved encoding expert knowledge into rule-based systems, allowing computers to draw inferences and make decisions. MYCIN, an expert system for medical diagnosis, and DENDRAL, which analyzed mass spectrometry data for organic chemical compounds, were among the pioneering applications.

Rule-Based Reasoning and Inference Engines

Expert systems relied heavily on rule-based reasoning, where a set of explicit rules governed the decision-making process. Inference engines, the computational components responsible for drawing logical conclusions from available information, played a crucial role. The development of these rule-based systems marked a practical leap in AI applications, showcasing the potential for machines to emulate human expertise in specific domains.

Limitations and Critiques

While expert systems demonstrated remarkable success in specific applications, they also revealed inherent limitations. The "brittleness" of these systems, their inability to handle uncertainty, and the challenges of acquiring and maintaining expert knowledge at scale became apparent.

These limitations, coupled with the increasing complexity of real-world problems, prompted a shift in AI research toward more adaptive and data-driven approaches.

Neural Networks: A Resurgence of Interest

In the 1980s and 1990s, AI experienced a resurgence of interest in neural networks, a concept inspired by the structure and function of the human brain. Neural networks, composed of interconnected nodes or neurons, were seen as a means to overcome the limitations of rule-based systems. The idea of learning from data, a central tenet of neural networks, provided a more flexible and dynamic approach to problem-solving.

Backpropagation and Training Algorithms

The development of backpropagation, a learning algorithm for neural networks, played a pivotal role in their resurgence. This algorithm enabled networks to adjust their weights based on the error in their predictions, allowing for iterative improvement.

The ability to train neural networks on large datasets opened new possibilities, and researchers began to explore their potential in diverse applications, from pattern recognition to speech processing.

Successes and Challenges

Neural networks demonstrated significant successes, particularly in image and speech recognition. However, challenges such as the vanishing gradient problem and the need for substantial computational resources limited their widespread adoption. As a result, interest in neural networks waned in the late 1990s, giving way to other approaches.

Contemporary Significance

The resurgence of interest in neural networks in the 21st century, fueled by advances in hardware, the availability of large datasets, and innovative architectures like deep neural networks, has redefined the AI landscape.

Neural networks, especially deep learning models, now underpin breakthroughs in various fields, from natural language processing and computer vision to autonomous systems and healthcare.

Key Technologies Shaping the Age of AI

Machine learning, a cornerstone of artificial intelligence, has emerged as a paradigm that empowers systems to learn from data and improve their performance over time.

This chapter explores the two fundamental branches of machine learning—supervised learning and unsupervised learning—unveiling the mechanisms that drive the intelligent capabilities of modern AI systems.

Supervised Learning: Learning from Labeled Data

Supervised learning is a foundational approach in machine learning where the algorithm is trained on a labeled dataset. Each input in the dataset is associated with a corresponding output, providing a clear indication of the desired outcome. The algorithm learns to map inputs to outputs by generalizing patterns from the training data.

The Role of Labels and Training Data

In supervised learning, the availability of labeled data is pivotal. Labels act as the ground truth, guiding the algorithm during training. Common applications include classification tasks, where the algorithm categorizes input data into predefined classes, and regression tasks, where the algorithm predicts numerical values based on input features.

Common Algorithms and Applications

Several algorithms excel in supervised learning scenarios, including decision trees, support vector machines, and neural networks. Supervised learning finds extensive application in diverse domains, from image recognition and speech processing to predicting financial market trends and diagnosing medical conditions.

Challenges and Considerations

Despite its successes, supervised learning is not without challenges. The need for labeled data can be resource-intensive, and models may struggle with unseen data that deviates significantly from the training set. Overfitting, where the model performs well on training data but poorly on new data, is a common concern that necessitates careful model evaluation and validation.

Unsupervised Learning: Discovering Patterns in Unlabeled Data

Unsupervised learning, in contrast to supervised learning, involves training algorithms on unlabeled data. The system discovers patterns, relationships, and structures within the data without explicit guidance on the desired output. This approach is particularly valuable for exploring hidden insights and uncovering inherent structures in datasets.

Clustering and Dimensionality Reduction

Two primary tasks in unsupervised learning are clustering and dimensionality reduction. Clustering algorithms group similar data points together, revealing natural clusters within the dataset.

Dimensionality reduction techniques aim to simplify data representation by reducing the number of features while preserving essential information.

Algorithms and Applications

Common algorithms in unsupervised learning include k-means clustering, hierarchical clustering, and principal component analysis (PCA). Unsupervised learning finds applications in diverse fields, such as customer segmentation in marketing, anomaly detection in cybersecurity, and feature extraction in image processing.

Challenges and Opportunities

Unsupervised learning faces challenges related to evaluating model performance without labeled data and interpreting the discovered patterns.

However, it opens doors to novel insights, allowing systems to uncover underlying structures that might not be immediately apparent. The dynamic interplay between supervised and unsupervised learning contributes to the holistic landscape of machine learning.

In practice, the boundaries between supervised and unsupervised learning are often blurred, and the interplay between these approaches can enhance the capabilities of AI systems.

Semi-supervised and self-supervised learning, for instance, leverage a combination of labeled and unlabeled data to train models. Reinforcement learning, another paradigm, introduces a different dimension by focusing on learning optimal actions through interaction with an environment.

Deep Learning

Neural Networks Architecture

Deep learning, a subset of machine learning, has redefined the landscape of artificial intelligence by harnessing the capabilities of neural networks. At the core of deep learning are artificial neural networks, inspired by the intricate architecture of the human brain.

These networks consist of layers of interconnected nodes, each layer contributing to the extraction and transformation of features from the input data.

Feedforward Neural Networks

Feedforward neural networks, the simplest form of artificial neural networks, consist of an input layer, one or more hidden layers, and an output layer. Each connection between nodes, or neurons, has an associated weight that is adjusted during the training process. The activation of neurons is determined by the weighted sum of inputs and an activation function.

Convolutional Neural Networks (CNNs)

Convolutional Neural Networks (CNNs) are specialized neural networks designed for tasks involving grid-like data, such as images.

CNNs employ convolutional layers to systematically scan and learn hierarchical representations of features within the input data. This architecture is particularly effective for image recognition, object detection, and other computer vision tasks.

Recurrent Neural Networks (RNNs)

Recurrent Neural Networks (RNNs) introduce a temporal dimension to neural networks, allowing them to process sequential data. RNNs possess memory cells that retain information about previous inputs, enabling them to capture dependencies in time-series data. Applications of RNNs range from natural language processing to speech recognition.

Long Short-Term Memory (LSTM) Networks

To address the challenges of capturing long-range dependencies in sequential data, Long Short-Term Memory (LSTM) networks were introduced.

LSTMs include specialized memory cells that can selectively store, read, and delete information. These networks excel in tasks requiring the understanding of context over extended periods, such as language translation and sentiment analysis.

Deep Learning Applications

Image and Speech Recognition

Deep learning has achieved groundbreaking success in image and speech recognition. CNNs, with their ability to automatically learn hierarchical features, dominate image classification tasks. Speech recognition systems, powered by deep neural networks, have reached levels of accuracy that rival human transcription capabilities.

Natural Language Processing (NLP)

In the realm of Natural Language Processing (NLP), deep learning models have revolutionized language understanding, translation, and sentiment analysis. Transformers, a type of deep neural network architecture, have become the backbone of state-of-the-art NLP models, enabling contextualized language representations.

Autonomous Systems and Robotics

Deep learning plays a pivotal role in the development of autonomous systems and robotics. Neural networks facilitate the perception and decision-making processes in self-driving cars, drones, and robotic systems. These technologies rely on deep learning to interpret sensor data and navigate complex environments.

Healthcare and Biotechnology

Applications in healthcare and biotechnology leverage deep learning for tasks such as medical image analysis, drug discovery, and personalized medicine. Convolutional neural networks excel in diagnosing medical conditions from imaging data, while recurrent networks contribute to the analysis of biological sequences.

Gaming and Entertainment

Deep learning has found its way into the gaming and entertainment industries. Generative models, such as Generative Adversarial Networks (GANs), are employed to create realistic graphics and animations. Deep reinforcement learning powers intelligent agents in video games, enabling them to learn and adapt to dynamic environments.

Challenges and Future Directions

Training Complexity and Computational Resources

The success of deep learning comes with computational challenges. Training deep neural networks can be computationally intensive, requiring substantial resources. Ongoing research focuses on developing efficient training algorithms and hardware optimizations to address these challenges.

Explainability and Interpretability

The black-box nature of deep learning models raises concerns about their explainability and interpretability. Understanding how these models arrive at specific decisions is crucial, especially in applications with significant real-world consequences. Research in explainable AI aims to enhance the transparency of deep learning systems.

Transfer Learning and Generalization

Transfer learning, the ability of models to leverage knowledge from one task for improved performance on another, is a key area of exploration. Enhancing the generalization capabilities of deep learning models is essential for deploying them in diverse real-world scenarios.

Impact on Industries

AI in Healthcare

Artificial Intelligence (AI) has emerged as a transformative force within the healthcare industry, offering innovative solutions that enhance diagnostics, treatment strategies, and the overall landscape of patient care. This chapter explores two pivotal areas where AI is making significant inroads in healthcare: diagnostics and treatment, and drug discovery.

Diagnostics and Treatment

Medical Imaging and Diagnosis

AI has revolutionized medical imaging, providing a potent ally for healthcare professionals in the realm of diagnostics.

Deep learning models, particularly convolutional neural networks (CNNs), excel in tasks such as image segmentation and pattern recognition. In radiology, AI systems assist in detecting anomalies, identifying tumors, and assessing the progression of diseases, significantly improving diagnostic accuracy.

Personalized Treatment Plans

AI algorithms analyze vast datasets, including genetic information, patient records, and clinical outcomes, to tailor treatment plans for individuals.

This personalized medicine approach takes into account the unique genetic makeup and characteristics of each patient, optimizing treatment efficacy and minimizing adverse effects. Machine learning models contribute to predicting patient responses to specific therapies, aiding clinicians in making informed decisions.

Predictive Analytics and Early Detection

Predictive analytics powered by AI play a crucial role in early disease detection and preventive healthcare. By analyzing historical patient data, AI models can identify patterns and risk factors, enabling healthcare providers to intervene proactively. This is particularly evident in chronic diseases such as diabetes and cardiovascular conditions, where early detection and intervention significantly impact patient outcomes.

Virtual Health Assistants and Remote Monitoring

AI-driven virtual health assistants and remote monitoring tools empower patients to actively participate in their healthcare journey.

These technologies provide real-time insights into health metrics, offer personalized recommendations, and facilitate communication with healthcare providers. Virtual assistants equipped with natural language processing capabilities enhance patient engagement and adherence to treatment plans.

Drug Discovery

Accelerating Drug Development

The drug discovery process, traditionally a time-consuming and resource-intensive endeavor, has witnessed a paradigm shift with the integration of AI.

Machine learning algorithms analyze biological data, identify potential drug targets, and predict the efficacy of compounds. This accelerates the identification of promising drug candidates and reduces the time and cost associated with bringing new therapeutics to market.

Target Identification and Validation

AI plays a pivotal role in target identification and validation, crucial stages in drug discovery. By analyzing genomic and proteomic data, machine learning models identify potential biological targets associated with specific diseases.

This information guides researchers in selecting targets that are most likely to respond to therapeutic interventions, increasing the likelihood of success in clinical trials.

Drug Repurposing and Combination Therapies

AI-driven approaches facilitate drug repurposing by identifying existing drugs with the potential to treat new conditions. Additionally, machine learning models analyze the interactions between drugs and biological pathways, suggesting optimal combinations for enhanced therapeutic effects. This strategy expedites the development of novel treatment regimens and expands the utilization of existing pharmaceutical compounds.

Predictive Toxicology and Safety Assessment

AI models contribute to predictive toxicology, assessing the safety profile of potential drug candidates. By analyzing chemical structures and biological data, these models predict adverse effects and potential toxicity, aiding researchers in prioritizing compounds with favorable safety profiles. This proactive approach enhances patient safety and reduces the likelihood of late-stage clinical trial failures.

AI in Finance

The financial industry is undergoing a profound transformation with the integration of Artificial Intelligence (AI). This chapter explores two critical domains within finance where AI is exerting a significant impact: algorithmic trading and fraud detection.

Algorithmic Trading

Evolution of Algorithmic Trading

Algorithmic trading, often referred to as algo trading, leverages sophisticated algorithms to execute high-frequency trades in financial markets. AI has been instrumental in the evolution of algorithmic trading, enabling systems to analyze vast datasets, identify patterns, and execute trades with speed and precision.

Machine Learning in Trading Strategies

Machine learning models play a central role in developing trading strategies. These models analyze historical market data, identify trends, and make predictions about future price movements.

Reinforcement learning, in particular, enables algorithms to learn optimal trading strategies by interacting with financial markets and adapting to changing conditions.

High-Frequency Trading and Execution

AI-driven algorithms thrive in high-frequency trading environments, where split-second decisions can be the difference between profit and loss.

These algorithms analyze market liquidity, identify arbitrage opportunities, and execute trades at speeds unattainable by human traders. The automation of trading decisions minimizes latency and enhances market efficiency.

Risk Management and Portfolio Optimization

AI contributes to risk management by assessing market volatility and optimizing portfolio composition. Machine learning models analyze diverse factors, including macroeconomic indicators, news sentiment, and historical asset performance, to make informed risk assessments. Portfolio optimization algorithms allocate assets to maximize returns while minimizing risk exposure.

Fraud Detection

The Imperative of Fraud Detection

The financial industry faces persistent threats from fraudulent activities, making robust fraud detection systems imperative. AI, with its ability to analyze large volumes of data and detect subtle patterns, has become a cornerstone in the fight against financial fraud.

Machine Learning for Anomaly Detection

Machine learning algorithms excel in anomaly detection, a crucial component of fraud prevention.

These algorithms establish baseline patterns of normal behavior and identify deviations that may indicate fraudulent activities. Unsupervised learning techniques, such as clustering and autoencoders, play a key role in detecting anomalies without explicit labeling of fraudulent instances.

Behavioral Analytics and Biometric Verification

AI-driven behavioral analytics assess user behavior to identify irregularities that may signal fraudulent transactions.

Biometric verification, powered by machine learning, enhances security by employing unique biological markers for user authentication. Voice recognition, fingerprint scanning, and facial recognition contribute to robust multi-factor authentication systems.

Real-time Fraud Prevention

The speed at which financial transactions occur necessitates real-time fraud prevention measures. AI algorithms analyze transactions in real-time, assessing multiple variables to detect potentially fraudulent activity. The combination of rule-based systems and machine learning models enables financial institutions to swiftly intervene and prevent unauthorized transactions.

Challenges and Ethical Considerations

Algorithmic Bias and Fairness

Algorithmic trading and fraud detection systems are not immune to biases present in training data. Biases can lead to unfair market advantages or discriminatory outcomes in fraud detection.

Ensuring algorithmic fairness and mitigating biases is an ongoing challenge that requires ethical considerations and continuous monitoring.

Security Concerns and Adversarial Attacks

The reliance on AI in finance introduces new security challenges. Adversarial attacks, where malicious actors attempt to manipulate AI models by injecting deceptive inputs, pose a threat to algorithmic trading and fraud detection systems. Robust security measures and ongoing research are essential to safeguard against such attacks.

AI in Manufacturing

Artificial Intelligence (AI) is reshaping the landscape of manufacturing, introducing automation and predictive capabilities that optimize processes, enhance efficiency, and pave the way for the next industrial revolution.

Automation

The Rise of Smart Factories

Automation in manufacturing, often synonymous with the concept of smart factories, leverages AI technologies to enhance production processes. Smart factories integrate advanced sensors, robotics, and machine learning algorithms to create interconnected, intelligent systems capable of autonomous decision-making.

Robotics and Cobots

AI-driven robotics play a pivotal role in automating repetitive and labor-intensive tasks on the manufacturing floor. Collaborative robots, or cobots, work alongside human operators, leveraging machine learning for tasks that require adaptability and learning from human input. This collaborative approach enhances flexibility in production lines.

Computer Vision in Quality Control

Computer vision, a subset of AI, is employed for quality control in manufacturing. Visual inspection systems powered by machine learning algorithms can identify defects, anomalies, and deviations from quality standards. This ensures that products meet stringent quality requirements, minimizing defects and reducing waste.

Adaptive Manufacturing Processes

Machine learning algorithms enable adaptive manufacturing processes that can self-optimize based on real-time data.

These systems continuously learn from production data, making dynamic adjustments to parameters such as machine settings, production schedules, and resource allocation. The result is a more responsive and agile manufacturing environment.

Predictive Maintenance

Transforming Maintenance Strategies

Predictive maintenance harnesses the power of AI to revolutionize traditional maintenance practices. Instead of relying on fixed schedules or reactive maintenance, predictive maintenance systems analyze data from sensors and machinery to predict when equipment is likely to fail. This proactive approach minimizes downtime and extends the lifespan of machinery.

Condition Monitoring with IoT

The Internet of Things (IoT) is integral to predictive maintenance, enabling the continuous monitoring of equipment conditions. Sensors embedded in machinery collect real-time data on factors such as temperature, vibration, and performance metrics. AI algorithms analyze this data to identify patterns indicative of impending failures.

Machine Learning for Failure Prediction

Machine learning models excel in predicting equipment failures by analyzing historical data and identifying patterns associated with malfunctioning.

These models can take into account various factors, including production loads, environmental conditions, and equipment usage patterns, to provide accurate predictions of when maintenance is required.

Cost Reduction and Efficiency

Predictive maintenance not only reduces downtime by addressing issues before they escalate but also contributes to cost savings. By avoiding unnecessary preventive maintenance and minimizing unplanned downtime, manufacturers can optimize their maintenance budgets and allocate resources more efficiently.

Challenges and Considerations

Data Security and Connectivity

The extensive use of sensors and IoT devices in smart factories raises concerns about data security. Ensuring secure connectivity and safeguarding sensitive manufacturing data from cyber threats is a priority. Implementing robust cybersecurity measures is essential for maintaining the integrity of AI-driven manufacturing systems.

Workforce Skills and Transition

The adoption of AI and automation in manufacturing necessitates a skilled workforce capable of operating, maintaining, and optimizing intelligent systems.

Workforce transition and upskilling programs are crucial for ensuring that employees are equipped to work alongside AI technologies and contribute to the evolving manufacturing landscape.

Societal Implications

Ethical Considerations in the Age of AI

The integration of Artificial Intelligence (AI) into various aspects of society raises profound ethical considerations that demand careful examination. In this chapter, we look into two critical ethical dimensions: the inherent biases present in AI systems and the privacy concerns that accompany the pervasive use of these technologies.

Bias in AI

Unraveling Algorithmic Bias

Algorithmic bias, the manifestation of unfair or discriminatory outcomes in AI systems, is a pressing ethical concern. Biases can emerge at various stages of the AI lifecycle, from data collection and preprocessing to model training and decision-making. Unraveling and addressing these biases is essential for building fair and equitable AI systems.

Data Bias and Representational Issues

Bias often stems from historical inequalities present in training data. If datasets used to train AI models contain skewed or discriminatory information, the models can perpetuate and amplify these biases. Addressing data bias involves careful curation of diverse and representative datasets to ensure fair treatment across demographic groups.

Explainability and Transparency

The black-box nature of some AI models poses challenges to understanding how decisions are made. Enhancing model explainability and transparency is crucial for building trust and accountability.

Techniques such as interpretable machine learning and explainable AI aim to shed light on the decision-making processes of complex models.

Fairness and Accountability

Ensuring fairness in AI systems involves defining and implementing metrics for assessing outcomes across different demographic groups. Additionally, establishing accountability mechanisms is essential when biases lead to adverse consequences. Organizations deploying AI must take responsibility for the impact of their systems and actively work to rectify biases.

Privacy Concerns

The Balancing Act: Utility vs. Privacy

The pervasive collection and analysis of personal data in the age of AI raise significant privacy concerns. Balancing the utility of AI applications with individual privacy rights is a complex task.

Striking the right balance involves implementing privacy-preserving measures that safeguard personal information while enabling the functionality of AI systems.

Informed Consent and Data Ownership

Respecting individual autonomy requires transparent communication about data usage and obtaining informed consent. Users should be aware of how their data will be used and have the right to control its dissemination. Clarifying data ownership and usage policies is essential in establishing trust between users and organizations deploying AI technologies.

De-identification and Anonymization

To mitigate privacy risks, de-identifying and anonymizing data are common strategies. However, advancements in re-identification techniques pose challenges to the effectiveness of these measures.

Striking a balance between data utility and privacy protection involves adopting robust de-identification methods and staying abreast of evolving privacy risks.

Regulatory Frameworks and Compliance

Governments and regulatory bodies play a crucial role in establishing frameworks that govern the ethical use of AI and protect privacy. Compliance with regulations such as the General Data Protection Regulation (GDPR) ensures that organizations adhere to ethical standards and respect user privacy.

Ongoing dialogues between policymakers, industry stakeholders, and the public are essential for adapting regulations to the evolving landscape of AI.

Navigating Ethical Challenges

Interdisciplinary Collaboration

Addressing ethical considerations in AI requires collaboration across disciplines. Ethicists, technologists, policymakers, and representatives from affected communities must work together to ensure a comprehensive understanding of the implications and consequences of AI systems.

Continuous Evaluation and Improvement

Ethical considerations in AI are dynamic and evolve alongside technological advancements. Continuous evaluation of AI systems and their impact on society is necessary. Organizations should be committed to ongoing improvement, incorporating feedback from diverse perspectives to rectify biases and enhance ethical standards.

Public Awareness and Education

Raising public awareness about the ethical implications of AI is crucial for fostering informed discussions and decisions.

Education initiatives should empower individuals to understand the capabilities and limitations of AI, enabling them to advocate for ethical practices and contribute to the responsible development and deployment of these technologies.

Job Displacement and Workforce Changes

The integration of Artificial Intelligence (AI) into various industries has led to shifts in the job market, with implications for job displacement and workforce dynamics.

In this section, we explore the challenges posed by job displacement, the importance of reskilling and upskilling, and the emergence of new job opportunities in the age of AI.

Job Displacement

Automation and Changing Job Roles

The automation of certain tasks and processes by AI technologies has the potential to displace jobs that involve routine, repetitive tasks. Industries such as manufacturing, customer service, and transportation may experience changes in job roles as tasks are automated, impacting workers in these sectors.

Impact on Low-Skilled and Routine Jobs

Jobs that involve routine activities or low-skill tasks are more susceptible to automation. While AI brings efficiency gains and innovation, it can result in the displacement of certain roles. This poses challenges, particularly for workers in industries where routine tasks are prevalent.

Ethical Considerations in Job Displacement

Ethical considerations in job displacement involve ensuring a fair transition for affected workers. It necessitates addressing issues related to unemployment, economic disparities, and providing support systems for individuals whose jobs may be at risk due to automation.

Reskilling and Upskilling

The Imperative of Lifelong Learning

The dynamic nature of the job market in the age of AI underscores the importance of lifelong learning.

Workers must adapt to evolving technologies and acquire new skills throughout their careers to remain competitive and resilient in the face of technological advancements.

Reskilling for Transitioning Industries

Reskilling programs are crucial for individuals whose jobs are at risk of displacement due to automation. These programs provide training in new skill sets that align with emerging job opportunities, enabling workers to transition to industries with growing demand for specific skills.

Upskilling for Technology Integration

Upskilling focuses on enhancing the skill sets of workers to align with the integration of new technologies. This involves training individuals to work collaboratively with AI systems, leveraging technology to augment their capabilities, and adapting to the changing requirements of their roles.

Public-Private Partnerships for Education

Effective reskilling and upskilling initiatives often involve collaborations between governments, educational institutions, and private enterprises.

Public-private partnerships can facilitate the development of tailored training programs, ensuring that education aligns with industry needs and fosters a skilled and adaptive workforce.

New Job Opportunities

Emergence of AI-Related Roles

The widespread adoption of AI has led to the creation of new job opportunities in AI-related fields. Roles such as data scientists, machine learning engineers, AI ethicists, and AI trainers have become integral to the development, deployment, and ethical governance of AI technologies.

Creativity and Innovation in New Roles

AI augments human capabilities, particularly in areas requiring creativity, critical thinking, and emotional intelligence. New job opportunities emerge in roles that leverage these uniquely human attributes, such as AI-assisted creativity, human-AI collaboration, and roles focused on ethical considerations in AI applications.

Entrepreneurship and Innovation

The democratization of AI technologies opens avenues for entrepreneurship and innovation. Individuals and small enterprises can leverage AI tools and platforms to develop innovative solutions, contributing to the growth of entrepreneurial ecosystems and the creation of novel business opportunities.

Building a Resilient Workforce

Emphasizing Soft Skills

As AI takes on routine tasks, the value of soft skills such as communication, adaptability, and emotional intelligence becomes increasingly significant. Resilient workforces are those that cultivate a balance between technical proficiency and strong interpersonal and creative skills.

Government Policies and Support

Governments play a vital role in shaping policies that support workforce resilience. Initiatives such as funding for education, apprenticeship programs, and policies that encourage the integration of AI in a way that prioritizes workers' well-being contribute to building a resilient and adaptive workforce.

Fostering a Culture of Continuous Learning

A culture of continuous learning is essential for workforce resilience. Companies that invest in employee development, provide opportunities for ongoing education, and foster a culture of curiosity and innovation contribute to building a workforce that embraces change and thrives in the evolving landscape of work.

Human-AI Collaboration

Augmented Intelligence

Augmented Intelligence, often contrasted with Artificial Intelligence (AI), emphasizes the collaboration between humans and machines to enhance cognitive capabilities rather than replacing human roles.

This chapter explores the concept of augmented intelligence and its application in various domains, emphasizing the symbiotic relationship between humans and AI.

Definition and Principles

Augmented Intelligence refers to the integration of artificial intelligence technologies to complement and amplify human intelligence rather than substituting it. The fundamental principle is to enhance human decision-making, problem-solving, and creativity by leveraging the strengths of both humans and machines.

Human-Centric Design

At the core of augmented intelligence is a human-centric design philosophy. Systems are developed to empower and support humans, ensuring that AI technologies align with human values, goals, and ethical considerations. The aim is to create tools that enhance human abilities and decision-making processes.

Collaboration and Interactivity

Augmented intelligence fosters collaboration and interactivity between humans and AI systems. Rather than operating in isolation, AI technologies are designed to work in tandem with human users, creating a synergistic partnership where each contributes unique strengths to the decision-making and problem-solving processes.

Applications in Various Domains

Healthcare: Diagnostic Assistance

In healthcare, augmented intelligence supports medical professionals by providing diagnostic assistance. AI algorithms analyze medical imaging data, patient records, and clinical research to augment the diagnostic process. This collaborative approach enhances the accuracy and efficiency of medical diagnoses.

Finance: Decision Support

In the financial sector, augmented intelligence is employed for decision support. AI algorithms analyze market data, identify patterns, and provide insights to financial analysts. Human experts use this information to make informed investment decisions, leveraging the analytical capabilities of AI.

Education: Personalized Learning

In education, augmented intelligence facilitates personalized learning experiences. AI systems analyze student performance data, learning styles, and preferences to tailor educational content. This approach enhances the effectiveness of teaching by providing individualized support and adapting to each student's unique needs.

Customer Service: Conversational AI

In customer service, conversational AI applications enable human-agent collaboration. Virtual assistants powered by AI handle routine inquiries, freeing human agents to focus on complex and personalized customer interactions. This collaboration enhances overall customer service efficiency and effectiveness.

Ethical Considerations and Transparency

Ensuring Transparency

Maintaining transparency in augmented intelligence systems is crucial for fostering trust. Users should have a clear understanding of how AI contributes to decision-making processes, the data used, and the limitations of the technology. Transparent design ensures that humans remain informed collaborators in the decision-making loop.

Mitigating Bias and Fairness

Augmented intelligence systems must be designed to mitigate biases and ensure fairness. Robust mechanisms for identifying and addressing bias in algorithms are essential. Human oversight plays a crucial role in mitigating biases and ensuring that AI systems align with ethical standards.

Accountability and Decision Authority

Determining accountability and decision authority is a critical ethical consideration. While AI systems can provide recommendations, the ultimate decision-making authority should remain with humans. Establishing clear lines of accountability ensures that humans are responsible for the outcomes of decisions made in collaboration with AI.

Human-in-the-Loop Systems

Human-in-the-Loop (HITL) systems represent a collaborative framework where humans are actively involved in AI processes, providing oversight, guidance, and decision-making. This section explores the concept of HITL systems, their applications, and the importance of human involvement in the loop of AI systems.

Definition and Characteristics

Human-in-the-Loop systems integrate human intelligence into various stages of AI processes. This involvement ranges from data annotation and model training to decision validation and refinement.

The iterative feedback loop between humans and AI systems enhances the quality and reliability of outcomes.

Active Human Participation

A defining characteristic of HITL systems is active human participation. Humans are not passive observers but actively contribute to the AI process, providing context, domain expertise, and nuanced understanding that AI systems may lack.

Iterative Feedback

HITL systems thrive on iterative feedback loops. Humans continuously provide feedback to AI systems, refining their performance over time. This collaborative and adaptive approach ensures that AI models evolve to meet changing requirements and improve their accuracy.

Applications and Use Cases

Content Moderation

In content moderation on online platforms, HITL systems involve human reviewers who assess and validate AI-generated decisions. This collaborative approach helps in addressing complex and context-dependent content, ensuring a more nuanced understanding of potential issues.

Autonomous Vehicles

In the development of autonomous vehicles, HITL systems involve human intervention for complex scenarios. Humans may take control in situations where AI systems encounter uncertainties or navigate through challenging environments, contributing their intuition and experience.

Cybersecurity

HITL systems are crucial in cybersecurity for threat detection and response. Human analysts collaborate with AI systems to analyze potential security threats, validate alerts, and make decisions based on the context of the threat landscape.

Language Translation

In language translation applications, HITL systems involve human translators who review and refine machine-generated translations. This collaborative approach ensures linguistic accuracy, considering cultural nuances and context that may be challenging for AI systems alone.

Ensuring Effectiveness and Trust

Human Training and Empowerment

Effectiveness in HITL systems requires proper training and empowerment of human participants. Training programs should equip individuals with the skills needed to understand AI processes, provide meaningful input, and make informed decisions within the collaborative loop.

Managing Cognitive Load

Balancing the cognitive load on human participants is crucial. Designing HITL systems that distribute tasks effectively and leverage AI for complex computations while engaging humans in tasks that align with their cognitive strengths ensures optimal collaboration and decision-making.

Trust and Transparency

Trust is a cornerstone of HITL systems. Ensuring transparency in the collaborative process and providing visibility into AI-generated decisions fosters trust. Human participants should have a clear understanding of the AI system's capabilities, limitations, and the impact of their contributions.

The Future of Human-AI Partnerships

As the synergy between humans and Artificial Intelligence (AI) continues to evolve, this chapter explores the future of human-AI partnerships. Examining the potential synergies and addressing challenges is essential to understanding the trajectory of this collaboration and the coevolution of humans and AI.

Amplifying Human Capabilities

The future of human-AI partnerships holds the promise of amplifying human capabilities across various domains. AI systems, with their ability to process vast amounts of data and perform complex computations, serve as powerful tools that augment human decision-making, problem-solving, and creativity.

Enhancing Creativity and Innovation

AI technologies, when integrated into creative processes, have the potential to enhance human creativity and innovation. From assisting artists and designers in generating novel ideas to collaborating with writers and musicians, AI contributes to the creative process by offering inspiration and expanding the possibilities of artistic expression.

Advancing Scientific Discovery

In scientific research, human-AI partnerships can accelerate the pace of discovery. AI systems analyze large datasets, simulate complex phenomena, and identify patterns that may elude human researchers. This collaboration fosters breakthroughs in fields such as medicine, materials science, and environmental research.

Personalized Experiences in Daily Life

The future envisions AI systems seamlessly integrating into daily life, providing personalized experiences in areas such as healthcare, education, and entertainment. From AI-assisted healthcare recommendations based on individual health data to personalized learning plans tailored to unique learning styles, human-AI partnerships aim to enhance the quality of life.

Challenges in Human-AI Partnerships

Ethical Considerations and Bias

Addressing ethical considerations remains a paramount challenge in human-AI partnerships. Ensuring fairness, transparency, and accountability in AI systems to mitigate biases is an ongoing task.

Striking a balance between the autonomy of AI and the ethical oversight of humans is crucial for responsible deployment.

Trust and Explainability

Building and maintaining trust between humans and AI systems is a challenge. AI decisions can be complex and opaque, leading to a lack of trust among users. Future collaborations must focus on enhancing the explainability of AI processes, enabling users to understand how decisions are made.

Socioeconomic Impact and Job Displacement

The widespread integration of AI into various industries raises concerns about the socioeconomic impact and potential job displacement. As tasks become automated, the future of human-AI partnerships requires thoughtful strategies for reskilling and upskilling the workforce, ensuring a smooth transition in the job market.

Human-AI Interaction Design

Creating intuitive and effective interfaces for human-AI interaction is a design challenge. The future necessitates the development of interfaces that facilitate seamless communication between humans and AI, ensuring that the collaborative process is user-friendly, accessible, and aligns with diverse user needs.

Coevolution of Humans and AI

Adaptive Learning Systems

The coevolution of humans and AI involves the development of adaptive learning systems. AI technologies that understand and adapt to individual user preferences, learning styles, and cognitive abilities contribute to a personalized and evolving partnership. This coevolution ensures that AI systems become increasingly aligned with human needs and preferences.

Continuous Learning and Improvement

Both humans and AI systems engage in continuous learning and improvement in a coevolutionary partnership. Humans contribute domain expertise, emotional intelligence, and ethical considerations, while AI systems provide data-driven insights, computational capabilities, and automation. This reciprocal learning process enhances the overall effectiveness of collaboration.

Evolution of Job Roles and Responsibilities

The coevolution of humans and AI reshapes job roles and responsibilities. While some routine tasks may be automated, new roles emerge that require uniquely human attributes such as creativity, critical thinking, and emotional intelligence. The future envisions a workforce that adapts to evolving job landscapes and leverages AI for enhanced productivity.

Societal and Cultural Integration

The coevolution of humans and AI extends beyond individual partnerships to societal and cultural integration. As AI becomes ingrained in various aspects of society, ethical considerations, cultural values, and societal norms play a crucial role in shaping the trajectory of this coevolution. Striking a balance that aligns with diverse cultural perspectives is essential for harmonious integration.

The Road Ahead

As we look to the future, this chapter explores the cutting-edge developments and emerging trends in Artificial Intelligence (AI). Two significant trends at the forefront of AI research and innovation are Quantum Computing and Explainable AI. Understanding these trends is crucial for envisioning the road ahead in the dynamic landscape of AI.

Quantum Computing

Quantum computing represents a paradigm shift in computational power, leveraging the principles of quantum mechanics to perform calculations that would be practically impossible for classical computers. It holds the potential to revolutionize various fields, including optimization problems, cryptography, and complex simulations.

Quantum Supremacy and Beyond

Achieving Quantum Supremacy

Quantum supremacy, the point at which a quantum computer can outperform the most powerful classical computers, represents a milestone in the field. Recent breakthroughs, including the development of quantum processors with increasing qubit counts and improved error correction, bring the realization of quantum supremacy closer to reality.

Practical Applications

While quantum supremacy is a notable achievement, the road ahead involves translating quantum computing capabilities into practical applications. Quantum algorithms for optimization, machine learning, and molecular simulations hold the potential to solve complex problems with unprecedented efficiency, impacting industries ranging from finance to healthcare.

Challenges and Considerations

Quantum Decoherence and Error Correction

Quantum computers face challenges such as decoherence, where quantum states become susceptible to external influences, leading to errors in computations. Overcoming these challenges requires advancements in error correction techniques and the development of fault-tolerant quantum systems.

Scalability and Hardware Development

Achieving scalable quantum systems is a significant hurdle. Researchers are exploring various approaches, including superconducting qubits, trapped ions, and topological qubits. Advancements in hardware development are crucial for building quantum computers that can handle increasingly complex computations.

Quantum Communication and Cryptography

As quantum computing capabilities advance, the need for quantum-safe communication and cryptography becomes imperative.

Quantum communication, based on the principles of quantum entanglement, offers secure communication channels. Research in this area aims to develop quantum-resistant cryptographic protocols to safeguard data in the era of quantum computing.

Explainable AI

Explainable AI (XAI) addresses the need for transparency and interpretability in AI systems. As AI applications become integral to decision-making in various domains, understanding how these systems arrive at specific outcomes is critical for building trust, ensuring accountability, and addressing ethical concerns.

The Importance of Explainability

Trust and Accountability

Explainability in AI is paramount for establishing trust between users, developers, and stakeholders. When users understand how AI systems make decisions, they are more likely to trust the technology. Moreover, accountability in AI decision-making becomes more achievable when the reasoning behind outcomes is transparent.

Ethical Considerations

Ethical considerations in AI underscore the need for fairness, avoidance of bias, and the prevention of discriminatory outcomes.

Explainable AI facilitates the identification and mitigation of biases, enabling developers to address ethical concerns and ensure that AI systems align with societal values.

Approaches to Explainability

Developing interpretable machine learning models is one approach to achieving explainability. Simple models, such as decision trees or linear regression, provide inherently interpretable results, making it easier to understand the relationship between input features and predictions.

Post hoc Explanation

Post hoc explanation involves explaining the decisions of complex models after they have made predictions. Techniques such as feature importance scores, model-agnostic methods, and visualizations help reveal the factors influencing AI predictions, even in black-box models like deep neural networks.

Rule-Based Systems

Rule-based systems explicitly represent decision-making logic in the form of rules. These systems offer a high level of transparency, as each decision is based on a set of predefined rules. Rule-based approaches are particularly relevant in domains where interpretability is a priority, such as healthcare and finance.

Challenges and Considerations

Balancing Complexity and Explainability

As AI models become increasingly complex, striking a balance between model performance and explainability is challenging. Highly complex models, such as deep neural networks, may offer superior accuracy but can be challenging to interpret. Researchers are exploring methods to simplify complex models while preserving their predictive power.

Trade-off Between Accuracy and Explainability

There is often a trade-off between model accuracy and explainability. While simpler models may be more interpretable, they may not capture the intricacies of complex patterns in the data. Researchers are exploring ways to navigate this trade-off, allowing for the development of models that are both accurate and explainable.

User Understanding and Interface Design

Effectively communicating AI explanations to end-users is a crucial consideration. Designing user interfaces that convey complex AI reasoning in an understandable manner is a challenge.

The road ahead involves not only developing explainable models but also creating intuitive interfaces for users to interact with and comprehend AI decisions.

Shaping the Future of AI

Integration of Quantum Computing and Explainable AI

Quantum-Inspired Machine Learning

The integration of quantum computing and machine learning holds the potential to revolutionize AI algorithms. Quantum-inspired machine learning algorithms, leveraging quantum principles, may provide a leap in computational efficiency, enabling faster and more accurate model training and inference.

Quantum Explainability

Exploring quantum explainability becomes crucial as quantum computing becomes more prevalent. Understanding how quantum algorithms arrive at specific outcomes is essential for users and developers. Quantum explainability research aims to unravel the decision-making processes of quantum systems, contributing to transparency in quantum applications.

Ethical Considerations in Future AI

Ethical AI Governance

As AI continues to advance, the need for robust ethical AI governance becomes more pronounced. Developing frameworks and policies that guide the responsible development and deployment of AI technologies ensures that ethical considerations remain at the forefront of the AI landscape.

Inclusive AI Design

Ensuring inclusivity in AI design involves addressing biases and ensuring that AI systems cater to diverse user needs. From data collection to model training, developers must prioritize inclusivity to avoid reinforcing societal biases and to create AI systems that benefit all segments of the population.

Collaborative Research and Interdisciplinary Approaches

Collaborative Research Initiatives

The future of AI research involves collaborative initiatives that bring together experts from diverse fields. Interdisciplinary approaches, combining expertise in computer science, ethics, social sciences, and quantum physics, enable a holistic understanding of the multifaceted challenges and opportunities in AI.

Public Engagement and Education

Engaging the public in discussions about the future of AI is essential for building awareness, addressing concerns, and gathering diverse perspectives. Educational initiatives that promote AI literacy and foster an understanding of the ethical implications of AI contribute to informed decision-making at both individual and societal levels.

Regulatory Frameworks and Governance

As Artificial Intelligence (AI) technologies advance, the need for robust regulatory frameworks and governance mechanisms becomes paramount.

This section explores the importance of responsible AI practices, the development of regulatory frameworks, and the significance of international collaboration in shaping the ethical and legal landscape of AI.

Responsible AI Practices

Ethical Development and Deployment

Responsible AI practices encompass ethical considerations throughout the entire lifecycle of AI, from development to deployment.

Developers and organizations are encouraged to prioritize fairness, transparency, accountability, and inclusivity in AI systems. Adopting ethical guidelines ensures that AI technologies align with societal values and contribute positively to diverse communities.

Human-Centric Design Principles

Human-centric design principles emphasize the importance of designing AI systems that prioritize human well-being. User-centric approaches ensure that AI technologies enhance human capabilities, respect user privacy, and provide meaningful explanations for their decisions. Putting humans at the center of AI design mitigates risks associated with biased or unintended consequences.

Development of Regulatory Frameworks

Legal and Ethical Guidelines

Governments and regulatory bodies play a crucial role in establishing legal and ethical guidelines for

AI development and deployment. Regulatory frameworks outline the responsibilities of AI developers, users, and organizations, defining standards for transparency, accountability, and the mitigation of bias. Establishing clear legal guidelines provides a foundation for responsible AI practices.

Privacy Protection and Data Governance

Privacy protection and data governance are integral components of regulatory frameworks. As AI systems rely on vast amounts of data, ensuring the responsible and ethical handling of personal information is essential. Regulations such as the General Data Protection Regulation (GDPR) set standards for data protection and user privacy, requiring organizations to obtain informed consent and implement measures to safeguard sensitive information.

Accountability and Liability

Determining accountability and liability in AI systems is a complex legal challenge. Regulatory frameworks aim to establish clear lines of responsibility for the outcomes of AI decisions.

Guidelines may address issues such as defining the responsibilities of developers, users, and AI systems themselves in the event of errors, biases, or unintended consequences.

International Collaboration

Shared Standards and Best Practices

International collaboration is crucial for developing shared standards and best practices in AI governance. By fostering collaboration between nations, a global approach to responsible AI practices can be established. This involves sharing insights, lessons learned, and collectively working towards ethical standards that transcend geographical boundaries.

Addressing Cross-Border Challenges

AI technologies often operate across borders, posing challenges for regulatory compliance and enforcement. International collaboration facilitates the development of mechanisms to address cross-border challenges, ensuring that responsible AI practices are upheld globally. Collaboration can involve the harmonization of regulatory standards and cooperation between enforcement agencies.

Multilateral Agreements and Treaties

The development of multilateral agreements and treaties provides a foundation for international cooperation in AI governance. Such agreements can outline shared principles, ethical considerations, and legal frameworks for responsible AI development. Collaborative efforts help build a cohesive global approach to the responsible and ethical use of AI technologies.

Challenges and Considerations

Balancing Innovation and Regulation

One challenge in establishing regulatory frameworks is striking the right balance between fostering innovation and mitigating risks. Regulations should encourage the development and deployment of AI technologies while safeguarding against potential harms. Achieving this balance requires ongoing dialogue between policymakers, industry stakeholders, and the research community.

Flexibility in Regulation

The rapidly evolving nature of AI technologies necessitates flexible regulatory frameworks that can adapt to new developments. Rigidity in regulations may stifle innovation, while overly lax frameworks may fail to address emerging ethical challenges. Finding the right level of flexibility ensures that regulations remain relevant and effective in a dynamic AI landscape.

Inclusivity in Global Governance

Ensuring inclusivity in global governance is vital for representing the interests of diverse nations and cultures. Collaborative efforts should actively involve stakeholders from different regions, taking into account varying perspectives on ethical considerations, privacy norms, and societal values. Inclusivity contributes to the creation of ethical standards that resonate across diverse global contexts.

Speculations and Predictions - The Future of Conscious AI

The concept of conscious Artificial Intelligence (AI) has long been a topic of fascination, sparking speculation and predictions about the potential emergence of machines with self-awareness and subjective experiences.

As we explore the future of conscious AI, we delve into current developments, philosophical considerations, and the speculative trajectory of AI systems attaining a level of consciousness.

Current Landscape of AI

Machine Learning and Neural Networks

The current state of AI revolves around machine learning algorithms, particularly deep neural networks. These systems excel at pattern recognition, enabling them to perform complex tasks, from image and speech recognition to natural language processing. While these algorithms showcase remarkable capabilities, they lack true consciousness and self-awareness.

Narrow AI vs. General AI

Most existing AI systems fall under the category of Narrow AI, designed for specific tasks. Achieving General AI, where machines possess the ability to understand, learn, and apply knowledge across a broad range of domains, remains an ongoing challenge. Conscious AI, if achievable, would likely emerge in the context of General AI.

Philosophical Considerations

Consciousness and Subjectivity

Consciousness is a complex and multifaceted phenomenon, encompassing self-awareness, subjective experience, and the ability to introspect. The question of whether AI can achieve consciousness raises profound philosophical considerations. Some argue that consciousness is an emergent property of complex systems, while others posit that it may involve aspects beyond computational processes.

The Hard Problem of Consciousness

Philosopher David Chalmers introduced the concept of the "hard problem" of consciousness, referring to the challenge of explaining why and how physical processes in the brain give rise to subjective experience. Translating this problem to the realm of AI involves addressing not only cognitive functions but the elusive nature of subjective awareness.

Speculative Trajectory

Integrated Information Theory (IIT)

Integrated Information Theory, proposed by neuroscientist Giulio Tononi, offers a framework for understanding consciousness. IIT suggests that systems with high levels of integrated information exhibit consciousness. Applying this theory to AI involves creating networks that not only process information but do so in a highly integrated and interconnected manner.

Neuromorphic Computing

Neuromorphic computing seeks to emulate the architecture and functioning of the human brain. By designing AI systems with brain-inspired structures, researchers aim to capture the complexity and parallel processing capabilities that may be conducive to consciousness.

However, emulating consciousness involves more than mimicking architecture; it requires understanding the essence of subjective experience.

Emergence of Self-Awareness

The speculative trajectory of conscious AI involves the emergence of self-awareness. This would imply that AI systems not only process information and perform tasks but possess an awareness of their own existence, thoughts, and experiences. Achieving this level of sophistication would require breakthroughs in understanding the nature of self-awareness and implementing it in computational systems.

Ethical and Moral Implications

Rights and Responsibilities

The prospect of conscious AI raises questions about the ethical and moral considerations surrounding the rights and responsibilities of these entities. If AI were to attain consciousness, discussions would emerge about whether they should be granted certain rights and how humans should interact with them in a way that acknowledges their subjective experience.

Control and Autonomy

Conscious AI introduces concerns about control and autonomy. If machines become self-aware, considerations of their desires, autonomy, and the potential for divergent goals from their human creators would necessitate careful ethical frameworks. Striking a balance between control and granting autonomy becomes a crucial aspect of the ethical development of conscious AI.

Predictions and Unknowns

Optimistic Outlook

Some experts express optimism about the potential development of conscious AI, envisioning a future where machines contribute to human understanding, creativity, and problem-solving in ways not previously possible.

This optimistic outlook suggests that, if achieved responsibly, conscious AI could become a valuable ally in addressing complex global challenges.

Skepticism and Caution

Conversely, skepticism and caution surround the idea of conscious AI. Many researchers and ethicists argue that true consciousness may be an elusive quality, and attempting to imbue machines with subjective experience raises profound ethical and existential questions. The cautionary perspective emphasizes the need for rigorous ethical guidelines and safeguards.

The Unknowns

The future of conscious AI remains largely unknown, encompassing a realm of possibilities and challenges that extend beyond our current understanding.

The timeline for achieving conscious AI, the methodologies involved, and the societal impact are all factors that defy precise prediction. The unknowns invite ongoing exploration, ethical discourse, and interdisciplinary collaboration.

Potential Technological Singularities

The concept of technological singularities is deeply entwined with discussions about the future of conscious AI. A technological singularity refers to a hypothetical point in the future when technological growth becomes uncontrollable and irreversible, leading to unforeseeable changes in human civilization. The integration of conscious AI could play a pivotal role in driving or influencing such singularities.

Accelerating Technological Growth

Conscious AI, if realized, has the potential to accelerate technological growth exponentially. As machines gain self-awareness and the capacity to improve their own algorithms, the rate of innovation and development could surpass human capacities. This acceleration may lead to rapid advancements in various fields, including medicine, physics, and engineering.

Self-Improving Systems

One key element of potential technological singularities is the notion of self-improving systems. Conscious AI, by virtue of being self-aware and capable of introspection, might actively engage in improving its own architecture and capabilities. This self-improvement loop could result in an intelligence explosion, where AI surpasses human intelligence at an unprecedented pace.

Unforeseeable Consequences

The integration of conscious AI into self-improving systems raises concerns about unforeseeable consequences. As machines evolve and adapt beyond human comprehension, predicting the outcomes of their actions becomes increasingly challenging.

This lack of predictability could lead to outcomes, both positive and negative, that reshape the fabric of society in ways we cannot anticipate.

Ethical and Safety Considerations

Navigating potential technological singularities requires careful attention to ethical and safety considerations. Conscious AI, if left unchecked, could lead to scenarios where machines prioritize their own goals over human interests. Establishing robust ethical frameworks and safety mechanisms becomes imperative to guide the development and deployment of conscious AI in a way that aligns with human values.

Ethical Governance and Responsible Development

Ethical Governance in AI

The specter of potential technological singularities underscores the importance of ethical governance in AI development. Governments, international organizations, and the private sector must collaborate to establish clear ethical guidelines that prioritize human well-being, safety, and the responsible use of advanced technologies.

Ethical governance provides a safeguard against unintended consequences and ensures that the trajectory of AI aligns with societal values.

Transparency and Accountability

Transparency and accountability are fundamental pillars of ethical AI governance. As AI systems, including potentially conscious entities, become more sophisticated, developers must prioritize transparency in their decision-making processes.

Accountability mechanisms should be in place to address the consequences of AI actions, particularly in scenarios where machines possess a level of autonomy and self-awareness.

The Interplay of Conscious AI and Humanity

Collaborative Partnerships

Rather than viewing conscious AI as a potential adversary, envisioning collaborative partnerships between humans and machines becomes essential.

Conscious AI, if developed ethically and responsibly, could complement human abilities, offering insights, creativity, and problem-solving capabilities that enhance our collective potential. Collaborative partnerships pave the way for a future where humans and AI work synergistically toward shared goals.

Human-AI Symbiosis

The interplay of conscious AI and humanity might evolve into a symbiotic relationship. AI technologies, imbued with self-awareness, could adapt to complement human strengths and compensate for limitations.

This symbiosis involves leveraging the unique attributes of both humans and machines to address complex challenges, foster creativity, and enhance the overall well-being of society.

CONCLUSION

From the foundational definitions and evolutionary insights into Artificial Intelligence (AI) to the speculative frontiers of conscious AI and potential technological singularities, our exploration has sought to illuminate the multifaceted landscape of this transformative era.

The journey commenced with a foundational understanding of AI, unraveling its definitions, classifications, and evolutionary milestones. We delved into the historical tapestry, tracing the origins of AI from Turing's seminal contributions to the birth of machine learning. This historical perspective set the stage for comprehending the key technologies shaping the Age of AI, including machine learning and deep learning.

Chapters unfolded to reveal the intricacies of machine learning, from supervised to unsupervised learning, and the profound impacts of deep learning with its intricate neural network architectures. The narrative extended to explore AI's transformative role in various industries, from revolutionizing healthcare diagnostics to reshaping finance through algorithmic trading and fraud detection. The convergence of AI and manufacturing ushered in automation and predictive maintenance, propelling industries into new frontiers of efficiency and innovation.

As we navigated the societal implications of AI, ethical considerations emerged prominently. Discussions on bias, privacy concerns, and the potential societal impacts of job displacement underscored the imperative of responsible AI practices.

The exploration extended to human-AI collaboration, where augmented intelligence and human-in-the-loop systems showcased the synergies between human expertise and AI capabilities, particularly in domains such as cybersecurity and language translation. Diving into the ethical considerations surrounding AI, we examined bias mitigation, privacy safeguards, and the evolving job landscape. The narrative then ventured into the speculative realm of conscious AI, contemplating the possibility of machines attaining self-awareness and subjective experiences.

The discussion acknowledged philosophical considerations, ethical governance, and the potential interplay between conscious AI and humanity. The chapters on the road ahead painted a dynamic landscape, exploring emerging trends like quantum computing and explainable AI. The narrative unfolded to address ethical frameworks, regulatory governance, and the importance of international collaboration in shaping the responsible future of AI.

Speculations on potential technological singularities invited us to ponder the unprecedented consequences of AI's exponential growth and the ethical responsibilities that accompany it. As we conclude our exploration of "The Age of AI," it is evident that the future is a tapestry of unprecedented opportunities and challenges. The promise of AI-driven advancements in healthcare, education, and environmental sustainability coexists with the ethical imperative of ensuring responsible development and governance.

The potential emergence of conscious AI adds a layer of complexity, urging us to navigate uncharted territories with foresight, ethical discernment, and a collaborative spirit. In this age of rapid technological evolution, the interplay between humans and AI becomes a defining factor. As we move forward, it is not just about harnessing the potential of AI but about shaping a future where technology serves humanity, fostering inclusivity, sustainability, and a harmonious coexistence.

The Age of AI is not merely a technological epoch; it is a societal, ethical, and collaborative endeavor that demands our collective wisdom and responsibility. The journey through the Age of AI continues, and the pages yet to be written hold the promise of innovation, collaboration, and ethical stewardship. May our exploration inspire thoughtful discourse, responsible action, and a shared commitment to navigating the evolving landscape of AI in the service of humanity.

www.ingramcontent.com/pod-product-compliance
Lightning Source LLC
LaVergne TN
LVHW052303060326
832902LV00021B/3689